How To Help Resolve
Your Family's Money Problems

**A Survival Skills Book
by Joy Berry**

Copyright © Joy Berry, 2020
Reprinted by permission. Originally Published 1990

The statements and opinions expressed in this work are solely those of the author and do not reflect the thoughts or opinions of the publisher.

Every effort has been made to trace the copyright holder(s) and obtain permission to reproduce all elements of this material.

All rights reserved. No part of this book may be reproduced or used in any manner without the prior written permission of the copyright owner, except for the use of brief quotations in a book review. For inquiries or to request permission, contact the publisher at rights@lemurpress.com

ISBN 978-1-63617-148-7

Published by Lemur Press
lemurpress.com

LEMUR PRESS

INTRODUCTION • 3

When your parents say, "We can't afford it," you need to know about the following:
- understanding family finances,
- dealing with financial problems,
- six ways to help your family, and
- working together on money problems.

4 ▪ INTRODUCTION

How do you feel when your parents tell you that they cannot afford to give you something you want?

When your family has money problems, do you sometimes feel frustrated and confused?

6 ▪ INTRODUCTION

When your parents tell you that you cannot have something because they cannot afford it, do you ever wonder...

INTRODUCTION ■ 7

This book tells you exactly why your parents might not be able to afford something. It also tells you what you can do to help resolve your family's money problems.

8 ▪ UNDERSTANDING FAMILY FINANCES

Every family has an **income.**

A family's income is the money it receives.

There are several ways a family can gather income:

- Family members can work and be paid for their work.
- Family members can sell things they own.
- Family members can receive interest on money they have saved or profits from money they have invested.
- Someone outside the family can give family members a gift of money.
- Someone in the family can receive an inheritance when a friend or relative dies.

10 ■ UNDERSTANDING FAMILY FINANCES

Every family has **expenses.**

Expenses are the things a family spends its income on.

Most families' expenses include
- food,
- shelter (house, apartment, or mobile home),
- utilities (water, gas, electricity, and garbage collection),
- telephone,
- transportation (car expenses, bus or train fare),
- clothing,
- medical bills (doctor, dentist, or orthodontist),
- taxes,
- insurance,
- repairs (on the family's home, car, or equipment),
- child care and education,
- donations,
- entertainment (hobbies, outings, or vacations), and
- miscellaneous items (gifts and other extras).

12 • UNDERSTANDING FAMILY FINANCES

A family's financial situation is acceptable when its **income is equal to its expenses.** When a family receives the same amount of money it spends, there is just enough money for what the family needs and wants.

UNDERSTANDING FAMILY FINANCES ▪ 13

A family's financial situation is more positive when its **income is greater than its expenses.** When a family receives more money than it spends, there is money left after the family has paid for what it needs and wants.

14 ▪ UNDERSTANDING FAMILY FINANCES

A family's financial situation is in trouble when **its income is less than its expenses.** When a family receives less money than it spends, there is not enough money to pay for what the family needs and wants.

UNDERSTANDING FAMILY FINANCES ■ 15

There are two main reasons why a family's income might be less than its expenses:

- The income stays the same while the expenses increase.
- The income decreases while the expenses stay the same.

16 ▪ UNDERSTANDING FAMILY FINANCES

There are several reasons that a family's expenses might increase:

- Inflation (a general rise in prices) can increase a family's expenses. One result of inflation is that everything a family needs or wants costs more.

UNDERSTANDING FAMILY FINANCES ▪ 17

- Changes in a family's needs or wants can cause its expenses to increase. If a family's needs or wants increase, its expenses will increase.

18 ▪ UNDERSTANDING FAMILY FINANCES

There are several reasons why a family's income might decrease:

A family's income might decrease if a family member's pay is cut (decreased).

UNDERSTANDING FAMILY FINANCES • 19

A family's income might decrease if a family member
- changes jobs and is paid less in the new job than in the old one, or
- loses his or her job.

20 ▪ DEALING WITH FINANCIAL PROBLEMS

The family's income will decrease if it stops receiving income from savings, investments, or gifts.

DEALING WITH FINANCIAL PROBLEMS ▪ 21

If there is not enough money for your family to buy all the things it needs and wants, you can be sure that your parents will respond to most of your requests for things you want by saying...

22 ▪ DEALING WITH FINANCIAL PROBLEMS

When your parents tell you that they can't afford what you want, you might feel **disappointed**.

DEALING WITH FINANCIAL PROBLEMS ▪ 23

Because you feel disappointed, you might want to **complain.**

24 ▪ DEALING WITH FINANCIAL PROBLEMS

When your parents tell you that they can't afford what you want, you might feel **frustrated.**

DEALING WITH FINANCIAL PROBLEMS ▪ 25

Because you feel frustrated, you might want to **nag** or possibly **throw a tantrum.**

26 ▪ DEALING WITH FINANCIAL PROBLEMS

When your parents tell you that they can't afford what you want, you might feel **cheated.**

DEALING WITH FINANCIAL PROBLEMS ▪ 27

Because you feel cheated, you might want to **threaten** or **badger** your parents to try to get them to buy what you want.

28 ▪ DEALING WITH FINANCIAL PROBLEMS

But complaining, nagging, threatening, or badgering your parents will not help.

Doing these things will not help increase your family's income. Doing these things will not decrease your family's expenses.

Complaining, nagging, threatening, or badgering your parents will only make things worse. Doing these things can cause your parents to feel guilty, hurt, and angry. Such feelings might hinder them from doing what they need to do to solve the problem.

30 ▪ SIX WAYS TO HELP YOUR FAMILY

You can help your parents instead of hindering them. Here are six ways you can help your parents when your family's finances are in trouble:

1. Be understanding.

Try to understand what your parents are going through.

SIX WAYS TO HELP YOUR FAMILY ▪ 31

If you try to be understanding, your attitude will improve. Then you will be able to give your parents the encouragement and support they need to solve the problem.

32 ▪ SIX WAYS TO HELP YOUR FAMILY

2. Be helpful.

Take care of yourself. Clean up after yourself. Help out any way you can around the house and yard.

SIX WAYS TO HELP YOUR FAMILY ▪ 33

If you do what you can to help out, your parents can spend more time doing what they need to do to earn the money the family needs.

34 ▪ SIX WAYS TO HELP YOUR FAMILY

3. Be careful, not wasteful.

Take care of your things and the things that belong to the family. Do not waste food or resources such as gas, electricity, and water.

If you take care of things, your family will not have to repair or replace them so often. If you are not wasteful, you can help your family save money.

36 ■ SIX WAYS TO HELP YOUR FAMILY

4. Stop careless spending.

Do not spend money on things such as junk food and toys, games, and extra clothes that you do not need.

Do not insist on going places and doing things that cost money. Learn to entertain yourself without spending money.

If you stop spending money carelessly, there will be more money to spend on the things you actually need.

38 ▪ SIX WAYS TO HELP YOUR FAMILY

5. Earn some money.

Look around your community. See if there is anything you can do to earn money.

The money you earn from any job you get will help you buy things your family might not be able to afford. Earning some of your own money can help your parents.

40 ▪ SIX WAYS TO HELP YOUR FAMILY

6. Get involved in your family's finances.

Talk with your parents about your family's income and expenses. Find out about your family's financial situation and offer to help in any way you can.

SIX WAYS TO HELP YOUR FAMILY ▪ 41

Offering to help will make you a part of the solution rather than a part of the problem.

42 ■ SIX WAYS TO HELP YOUR FAMILY

Here is a game you can play that will help you understand your family's finances:

This is what you will need to play the game:
- play money (you can buy it or make it yourself),
- a record of your family's income for one month, and
- copies of your family's bills for one month.

This is how to play the game:

- Count out enough play money to equal the family's total income for one month.
- Lay out all the bills so that they can all be seen.
- Count out the amount of play money needed to pay each bill.
- Put the correct amount of play money with each bill.
- If there is money left after all the bills have been paid, count whatever money remains. If you run out of money before all the bills have been paid, add up the bills that remain.

44 ▪ SIX WAYS TO HELP YOUR FAMILY

After you have played the game, discuss these questions with your parents:
- Is the income greater than the expenses?
- If the income is greater, what should be done with the money that is left over after the expenses have been paid?
- Are the expenses greater than the income?
- If so, what should be done to take care of the additional expenses?

SIX WAYS TO HELP YOUR FAMILY ■ 45

- What can be done to increase the income?
- What can be done to decrease the expenses?

46 ■ WORKING TOGETHER ON MONEY PROBLEMS

Remember, no two families are the same. Each one is different.

If you start comparing your family's financial situation with those of other families, you might begin to compete with them. Competing with other families might take your attention away from your own family and keep you from doing whatever is necessary to solve your family's money problems.

WORKING TOGETHER ON MONEY PROBLEMS ▪ 47

It might help you to remember that all families, no matter what their situations are, have things they can be thankful for.

Also, all families, no matter who they are, have problems to solve.

Successful families are ones that are thankful for what they have and that are committed to solving their problems.

Mutual support, love, and understanding can help families solve their problems.

48 ■ CONCLUSION

You can help improve your family's financial situation. And when you do, you will help cut down on the number of times your parents have to say, "We can't afford it!"

www.ingramcontent.com/pod-product-compliance
Lightning Source LLC
Chambersburg PA
CBHW081408070526
44583CB00020B/2720